This Is the Way
We Make Our Cookies

A Traditional Song
Adapted by Alan Trussell-Cullen

Dominie Press, Inc.

Publisher: Christine Yuen
Series Editors: Adria F. Klein & Alan Trussell-Cullen
Editor: Bob Rowland
Photographer: Simon Young
Designers: Gary Hamada & Lois Stanfield

The text in *This Is the Way We Make Our Cookies* is adapted from "The Mulberry Bush," a traditional children's song.

Published by:

๏ Dominie Press, Inc.

1949 Kellogg Avenue
Carlsbad, California 92008 USA

www.dominie.com

ISBN 0-7685-0612-3

Printed in Singapore by PH Productions Pte Ltd

3 4 5 6 PH 07 06

Table of Contents

This is the way we make our cookies!

Make our cookies!

Make our cookies!

This is the way we make our cookies,

on a bright and sunny morning!

This is the way we make our cookies!

Make our cookies!

Make our cookies!

This is the way we make our cookies,

on a bright and sunny morning!

This is the way we mix our cookies!

Mix our cookies!

Mix our cookies!

This is the way we mix our cookies,

on a bright and sunny morning!

keep clear of
moving machinery

10

This is the way we mix our cookies!

Mix our cookies!

Mix our cookies!

This is the way we mix our cookies,

on a bright and sunny morning!

This is the way we bake
our cookies!

Bake our cookies!

Bake our cookies!

This is the way we bake
our cookies,

on a bright and sunny
morning!

14

This is the way we bake our cookies!

Bake our cookies!

Bake our cookies!

This is the way we bake our cookies,

on a bright and sunny morning!

16

This is the way we eat
our cookies!

Eat our cookies!

Eat our cookies!

This is the way we eat
our cookies,

on a bright and sunny
morning!

Picture Glossary

bake:

eat:

mix:

Index